THE NIGHT OF THE SEA TURTLE

Lynn M. Stone

THE ROURKE CORPORATION, INC.
Vero Beach, FL 32964

Photo Credits:

All photos © Lynn M. Stone.

Library of Congress Cataloging in Publication Data

Stone, Lynn M.
    The night of the sea turtle / by Lynn M. Stone
        p. cm. – (Animal odysseys)
    Includes index.
    Summary: Describes the life and habitats of the loggerhead turtle.
    ISBN 0-86593-102-X
    1. Sea turtles – Juvenile literature. [1. Loggerhead turtle. 2. Sea turtles. 3. Turtles.] I. Title. II. Series: Stone, Lynn M. Animal odysseys.
    QL666.C536S76 1991
    597.92–dc20

                                        90-40268
                                            CIP
                                             AC

CONTENTS

1 A WINDOW TO THE PAST

You probably never thought of the seashore as a time machine, a window to the ancient past. But it can be. If

you have a little imagination, the seashore can send you on a trip millions of years back into time. On special summer nights when the great loggerhead sea turtles crawl onto certain beaches in the American Southeast, you can experience the Age of Dinosaurs.

Above:
Ghost crabs shuffle across the beach shells.

Let's take a walk on one of these beaches in Florida on a late summer night. The air is warm and humid, and your skin begins to feel damp, like a frog's. The beach plants, several steps above the sea's edge, are deep in shadow. The beach plum and sea grape bushes look the

5

Left:
The yellow-crowned night heron leaves its leafy perch to hunt on the night beaches.

same. The sea oats are easier to reckon with. Their long, graceful stems are silhouetted against the sky.

The moon's up, making things a little easier to see. But what's that clacking sound you hear on the shells? Moonlight or not, you can't quite see the ghost crab shuffling over the **wrack**, the ribbon of shells and seaweed left by the tide. The ghost crab lives in a beach burrow. At night the crab looks for little animals, dead or alive.

The moon casts a long, bright beam over the ocean. You notice other lights on the ocean. A long way off, a ship's light winks. Closer to shore, you can see glitter on the ocean, as if someone had scattered the sequins from a dress. That's **phosphorescence**, light produced by tiny particles in the water.

You hear another ghost crab, and this time you catch a glimpse of its sideways shuffle. Still, it's not much more than a shadow. A night heron, looking for ghost crabs, squawks. Startled by your approach, it flaps off into the darkness.

Waves slosh ashore. They're hushed tonight – the ocean is barely rumpled. Somehow, even though it's nighttime, the ocean soothes instead of threatens. It isn't casting much onto the shore, least of all sea monsters. But ahead of you, perhaps 100 paces, is something on the beach. It's impossible to know what it is, but it is, clearly, *something*.

It is a lump, and it is darker than the rest of the beach. Your eyes don't work nearly as well at night as an owl's eyes or the bulging eyes of the night heron, but you know that something is there. Your urge is to quicken your step, but the young woman from the Florida Nature Conservancy who is your guide quietly cautions you to wait. You wait for what seems like hours. Then the "lump" begins, slowly, to move higher onto the beach.

Right:
Florida State Park rangers lead turtle walks at Sebastian Inlet State Recreation Area on the Atlantic coast.

You're lucky. You've found a giant loggerhead sea turtle *(Caretta caretta)* crawling from the ocean onto the beach. Its kind have been doing the same thing for millions of years. One of its ancestors, known to scientists as *Archelon*, may have been crawling from the sea to lay eggs as many as 90 million years ago. That was back in the Age of Dinosaurs. Dinosaurs, like turtles, were **reptiles**. The dinosaurs disappeared, as you know, but the sea turtles have survived these millions of years. This beach is, indeed, a time machine.

Sea turtles are amazing creatures. They had something that the dinosaurs didn't – the means for survival on a changing earth. Fifty years ago one observer of turtles wrote, "Because they are still living, turtles are commonplace to us. If they were extinct," he continued, "their shells. . .would be a cause for wonder."

Now, with proper planning, you can take a night walk and see a giant sea turtle. You may not actually witness it crawl from the edge of the sea. But at many

beaches in the Southeast, you can watch a loggerhead sea turtle hard at work as she lays her eggs in the sand, just as her ancestors did on sandy beaches millions of years ago.

People in growing numbers have become interested in the welfare of **marine**, or sea, turtles. The quiet and respectful watching of sea turtles on the beach has become a popular activity in Florida.

For Americans, the term "sea turtle" usually means a loggerhead turtle. Few sea turtles of other species nest in the United States.

It might be difficult to understand why people want to help protect a hard, crusty, cold-blooded animal with a brain the size of a pecan. But consider what Dr. Archie Carr once said. Until his death in 1989, Dr. Carr was a long-time booster of sea turtle conservation and an expert on sea turtles. He explained his own early interest in sea turtles when he said, "I was drawn to sea turtles partly because. . .there were blank places in their known natural history, partly because I saw a hawksbill turtle come ashore out of phosphorescent surf one night and dig in the sand while a thin moon climbed."

Essentially Dr. Carr was saying that he found sea turtles both mysterious and fascinating. Most people don't go on to study sea turtles and write books about them, as Archie Carr did, but many people share his fascination with the mysterious creatures.

2 THE LOGGERHEAD AND ITS KIN

The loggerhead is one of five species of sea turtles found in the offshore waters of the United States. Generally, all these turtles live only in the warm ocean waters of the Southeast, although strays are found elsewhere.

The loggerhead, hands down, is the most common sea turtle in U.S. waters. It is also the only sea turtle that commonly nests on U.S. shores. But the loggerhead is not an all-American turtle by any means. Like most of the sea turtle species, loggerheads are widely distributed throughout the warm oceans of the world. The broad area in which they live is their **range**. The range of the loggerhead includes the warmer regions of the Pacific, Atlantic, and Indian Oceans, and the Mediterranean Sea. In the Americas, loggerheads normally range from Virginia south to Argentina. Summer stragglers turn up as far north as Canada's Atlantic coast.

Not all groups, or populations, of loggerheads throughout the world are identical. Groups are distinguished by differences in size, color, and perhaps habits. Scientists aren't sure how many different groups of loggerheads exist, but they do consider Pacific loggerheads distinct from Atlantic loggerheads. Pacific loggerheads range from southern California to Chile. These loggerheads do not breed in the United States, and they are rarely seen north of southern California.

The loggerhead is sometimes found in waters considered too cold for sea turtles. But unlike its relatives, the loggerhead is capable of living for short periods in comparatively cold water. Occasionally a loggerhead is stunned or even killed by rapidly cooling sea water, but scientists have discovered that loggerheads usually avoid the killing effects of cold water. Their bodily functions slow down and they become slow-moving. They eventually enter a sleeplike state similar to hibernation. They sometimes lodge themselves under rocks for a few days or even weeks. When the water warms, they become active again.

All sea turtles are similar in shape. They have long, smooth, gently rounded upper shells, called **carapaces**. They also have four broad, flattened flippers and large heads. All have hard shells except the leatherback turtle *(Dermochelys)*. The leatherback has a flexible, leathery carapace.

The loggerhead can be distinguished from its cousins by its blocklike head. It can also be identified by

Above:
The loggerhead's big, blocklike head helps distinguish it from its marine turtle relatives.

certain other characteristics. For instance, the loggerhead has a different number and arrangement of bony plates on its upper body than other marine turtles.

None of the sea turtles is colorful, but loggerheads, especially young specimens, are attractive. A loggerhead has a dark, brownish carapace. It has brown, yellow, and white trim on its head, neck, and flippers. Many old loggerheads have clusters of tiny, crusty **barnacles** attached to them.

There are some fundamental differences among the five sea turtle species. Ridley *(Lepidochelys)* turtles nest in large numbers close to each other on the same beach. Hawksbill turtles *(Eretmochelys)* nest apart from each other and often use rockier beaches than other sea turtles.

The loggerhead and Atlantic ridley turtles are **carnivores**; they eat marine animals. The leatherback and hawksbill eat animal and plant material. That eating habit makes them **omnivores**. The green turtle *(Chelonia)* lives mostly on marine grasses, one of which is turtlegrass. Because it is a plant eater, the green turtle is **herbivorous**.

Marine turtles also have different comfort zones. Some prefer deeper water than others, and some prefer warmer water. Other differences in marine turtles are being studied by **herpetologists**, the scientists who study reptiles.

By most standards, loggerheads are truly giant turtles. Nesting loggerheads of the Southeast usually weigh between 200 and 300 pounds. They have a carapace length of about 30 inches. Specimens over 300 pounds are unusual, but loggerheads in the 500- to 800-pound range have been recorded.

Loggerheads are much larger than the familiar freshwater turtles of ponds, rivers, and streams, of course. They are larger than hawksbills and ridleys, too. Generally, loggerheads and green turtles are about the same size. The champion heavyweight among the marine turtles is the leatherback. Leatherbacks, which are rarely seen in the United States, commonly weigh 600 pounds. They have reportedly topped 1,500 pounds.

Herpetologists don't know exactly where the loggerheads that nest in the United States spend most of their lives. Their on-shore time represents a tiny fragment of their lives. But herpetologists do know that loggerheads are capable of traveling long distances at sea. Loggerheads tagged with plastic discs on Florida beaches have been found in Chesapeake Bay, the Bahama Islands, and Mexico. An Australian researcher reported a loggerhead that had traveled over 1,200 miles in 62 days.

A loggerhead can swim long distances because it is beautifully **adapted**, or suited, to its ocean home, or **habitat**. It has a lightweight, streamlined carapace. Its flippers are paddlelike, and it is a powerful, agile swimmer. The loggerhead sleeps, mates, feeds, and spends virtually its entire life at sea. Adult males are as much a part of the ocean as salt. As far as is known, they never come ashore.

A loggerhead turtle does quite well without a sail or motor. Its swimming is powered by its long, front flippers. The turtle pumps those flippers up and down as if they were wings. The hind flippers aren't helpful for power, but they help steer the turtle just as a rudder steers a ship.

The strength for pumping the flippers comes from large pectoral muscles. Nature worked out a trade when it gave sea turtles large muscles at the base of their front flippers. In exchange for these muscles, the sea turtle gave up the ability to withdraw its head under its carapace. Freshwater turtles have retractable heads and necks. When threatened, the turtles pull in their heads. Sea turtles have no place for the head to withdraw to. Muscle occupies space which might otherwise be used as a "closet" in which to hide the head.

The loggerhead's big head and jaws are used to eat sponges, shellfish, and jellyfish, the loggerhead's natural **prey**. Adult loggerheads, in turn, are occasionally attacked by sharks. Nesting loggerheads frequently show

Above:
Pumping its long, front flippers like wings, a loggerhead propels itself in its marine habitat.

16

the scars of shark attack – missing or torn flippers. Other natural enemies of adult loggerheads are tiny, even invisible. They include certain marine **parasites** and probably the organism that causes red tide.

Red tide is the nickname for an overabundance of one type of tiny marine plant. When these tiny plants bloom in excess in the ocean, they create poisons that kill many kinds of sea animals. Charles LeBuff, director of Caretta Research, a marine turtle conservation organization, recalls several loggerheads strewn along Sanibel Island, Florida, after a severe red tide. Scientists who examined the turtles found that they had eaten large quantities of pen shells. The pen shells had been infected by the poisonous red tide organisms.

No one knows how deep a loggerhead can dive to feed. One loggerhead, however, was caught in a net 300 feet under water. That is the distance of a football field, from goal line to goal line. Loggerheads may be able to plunge even deeper. Leatherbacks are known to reach depths of 1,400 feet.

The characteristics that make the loggerhead wonderfully suited for the marine world don't help it on shore. Flippers are poor substitutes for legs on a beach. And a head that can't be tucked away in a body that can't walk, much less run, is exposed to great danger on land. No wonder that the loggerhead steals ashore only to lay her eggs.

3 NIGHT OF THE SEA TURTLE

Nesting begins on a late spring or summer night. The turtle cautiously crawls from the ocean onto a sandy beach. On shores where there is a large difference between the ocean's tides, the turtle usually "rides" in on a high tide. If she is not frightened by noise or lights or confronted by a concrete sea wall, the turtle will crawl from the sea's edge to the dry upper beach.

Left:
If she is not frightened by lights or noise, the loggerhead will crawl from the sea's edge to the upper beach.

The exact site of a loggerhead's nest may depend on the temperature of the sand, according to herpetologist Dr. Jim Richardson. His studies suggest that the female turtle feels sand with her throat sac. She digs her nest when she locates a sharp rise in sand temperature in the dry beach zone. Other factors may also influence the nest site – how compact the sand is, its salt content, moisture, and smell.

Right:
The loggerhead scoops a bulb-shaped nest hole with her hind flippers.

If for some reason the beach is not to her liking, she doesn't lay her eggs. She simply returns to the ocean, leaving behind a trail called a "false crawl." If she is satisfied with the beach, she shapes a shallow body pit in the sand. Then she scoops a bulb-shaped nest hole with her hind flippers. Her eggs, like slick, leathery golf

balls, soon begin tumbling from her **ovipositor** into the nest hole. Jaws slightly apart, the turtle sighs and lifts her head slightly with each ejection of eggs. Meanwhile, glands near her eye orbits drip a liquid that rids her of too much body salt and rinses sand away. Her "tears" and sighs gave rise long ago to the idea that she was crying in her labor. Certainly she does shed tears, but not because she feels sad.

Above:
Eggs the size of golf balls tumble from the turtle's ovipositor into the nest.

20

Above:
Sighs and "tears" are part of the egg-laying process for a mother loggerhead.

Natural causes take a severe toll of loggerhead eggs and hatchlings. The loggerhead helps make up for that loss by laying an average of 100 eggs per nest. Loggerheads usually nest every two or three years. They rarely nest in two consecutive seasons. During those

21

Left:
The logger-head's "tears" eliminate excess body salt and wash sand from her eyes.

years that she does nest, the female loggerhead may nest as many as seven times, most often at 12-day intervals. A tagged loggerhead that dug six nests on Sanibel Island deposited 920 eggs altogether. Despite such huge egg production by loggerheads, best guesses are that only a tiny fraction – perhaps one percent – of those eggs become mature turtles.

Below:

After laying her eggs, the loggerhead's flippers sweep sand over the nest site.

After laying her **clutch**, the loggerhead fills in the nest hole with her hind flippers acting like little shovels. She sweeps the nest site with her long, front flippers. Her efforts don't hide the fact that something large has

disturbed the sand. But the exact site of the nest hole is well hidden. When she begins crawling back to the sea, she leaves a tractorlike path. That trail in the sand will last for many hours. In the morning, beachcombers will notice the curious pathway in the sand. Some will wonder if a miniature tank had rolled on the beach and left the trail.

The loggerhead is adapted to life on solid ground about as well as a walrus is adapted to flight. Her departure from the beach seems painfully slow and awk-

Above:
The loggerhead's tractor tread path lingers in the sand the next morning.

Right:
A loggerhead's return to the sea is awkward and slow.

ward. Her weight on the sand creates pressure on her lungs. She stops frequently to lift her head and draw oxygen into her lungs. When she reaches the moist, crushed shells at the edge of the sea, her **odyssey** ashore ends. The lip of a wave splashes across her head. Her

spirit renewed, she slips into the surf. Floating now, buoyant like a cork, she quickly vanishes in the sea foam.

    With her return to the ocean, a loggerhead's term as "mom" is over. It has lasted only for as long as she was on the beach, about one hour. After the last sweep of

Above:
Odyssey over, a loggerhead reaches the comfort and familiarity of its ocean home.

sand has passed over her nest, she leaves the clutch of eggs forever. The eggs are unguarded.

Just how long before nesting a female loggerhead mates with a male, or males, is unknown. It seems likely, however, that loggerheads observe a mating season and that mating occurs a fairly short time before nesting. Loggerheads in the Southeast usually nest between late April and late August. Peak activity is in June and July.

The loggerhead nests in North America along the Atlantic seaboard and Gulf of Mexico states, from New Jersey to Texas, but rarely north of North Carolina. The greatest numbers of loggerheads are at Cape Romain, South Carolina, and on the Florida east coast from Cape Canaveral south to Jupiter Island. Jekyll and Little Cumberland islands in Georgia also have large concentrations of loggerheads.

At some Georgia and Florida parks and reserves, rangers lead groups of visitors on turtle walks. These nighttime prowls, like those at Sebastian Inlet State Recreation Area and Blowing Rocks Nature Preserve on the Florida east coast, are an ideal way to see turtles and learn more about them. Once egg-laying begins, loggerheads pay no attention to quiet human observers.

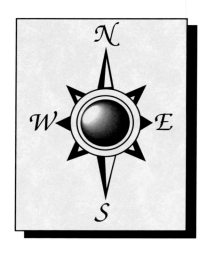

4
SURVIVING IN THE SAND

Forget Aesop's fable about the turtle beating the hare in a race. In reality, betting on a turtle to outrace a rabbit isn't smart. Likewise, a bet on a loggerhead turtle nest surviving storms, predators, human traffic, and the turtle's own mistakes isn't much wiser a bet.

Left:
The roots of the graceful sea oats can invade a turtle nest and destroy eggs.

Above:
Raccoons have an uncanny knack of finding and unearthing loggerhead nests.

Sometimes a clutch of eggs is laid too close to the ocean. A nest like this is quickly swamped by sea water. Even nests well above the sea's normal reach may be destroyed by salt water if a violent storm springs up. Nests can also be destroyed by the probing roots of sea oats or too much activity on the beach. If sand becomes too packed from people tromping on it or cars driving on it, the eggs become sealed in a tomb of sand.

Loggerhead nests that avoid those hazards may be dug up by predators – foxes, skunks, ghost crabs, hogs, and raccoons. Among these egg hunters, the greatest threat to loggerheads in the Southeast is the raccoon.

This furry, black-masked creature has such keen senses that it can find turtle nests when other animals can't. On turtle egg hunts, the raccoon apparently notices the loggerhead's trail in the sand and the shallow body pit. Scientist Rhett Talbert, who has studied raccoon activity on beaches in South Carolina, thinks that raccoons have exceptional senses of smell. Talbert suggests that perhaps raccoons can smell the lingering odor of turtle eggs. More likely, he says, raccoons smell the fluid which the turtle drips to help the eggs drop easily.

On Caladesi Island, Florida, turtle researchers found that raccoons were helping themselves to loggerhead nests as fast as the eggs were laid. At Cape Romano, Florida, and Kiowah Island, South Carolina, researchers discovered – probably to their horror – that raccoons were gobbling up as much as 95 percent of the loggerhead eggs.

Raccoons have always preyed on turtle eggs, but probably not to the extent that they do now. Today there are far more raccoons than before. Changes in the natural environment by man have helped raccoons in many places.

On Manasota Key, a wisp of island near Venice, Florida, the raccoon has a defender. Raccoons there turn up their noses at turtle eggs, according to Jane Fitzhugh, a former resident of the island. She offers the explanation that Manasota Key raccoons have been bought off or bribed. "People feed 'our' raccoons," she says, "so they don't know what a turtle egg is!"

Because of the dangers to which loggerhead nests are exposed, it has been a common practice for conservation personnel to relocate nests that seem threatened. People also gather and incubate eggs and, in some cases, "head start" hundreds of young turtles. They do this by keeping turtles in captivity until they seem large enough to no longer attract predators that would eat hatchlings. Headstarting raises the question of whether these turtles have been properly **imprinted** to their home beach, if imprinting occurs at all. And, having been raised by hand, can they survive in the wild on a natural food supply?

Imprinting is a process by which animals at birth, or shortly afterward, form an attachment to someone or something. Baby geese and cranes, for example, will develop an attachment toward a person if the person takes the place of the baby bird's parent. Animals can also be imprinted, or bonded, to an area, although how this occurs is not always clear.

5
RACE TO
THE SEA

Fifty to 60 days after the eggs are laid, loggerhead hatchlings emerge from the sandy nest at night. Usually the hatch is between 10 p.m. and midnight.

Below: *A few tiny heads poke like gray fingers through the sand as loggerhead hatchlings begin to emerge.*

Above:
The baby loggerheads erupt in a swarm from their nest.

The first clue that the turtles will soon hatch is a slight depression in the sand. As the activity of the hatchlings underground increases, sand slips downward in the nest hole. By collapsing to the bottom of the nest, falling sand may help create a "step" and raise the young turtles to the surface. Eventually, a few tiny heads poke like gray fingers through the sand. Then flippers appear,

33

and soon the tiny hatchlings, each of which is less than two inches long, erupt in a swarm. Within three minutes of the appearance of the first turtle's head, the nest is emptied.

Immediately after battling to the surface, the little turtles steer a fast course to the sea's edge – if there are no artificial lights to distract them. It is amazing that baby sea turtles on dark beaches race directly toward the sea. After all, they have never seen the ocean, and they could run in the opposite direction. But their ocean-finding system works beautifully.

Below:
Baby logger-heads hatch at night and immediately steer a fast course for the sea's edge.

The life histories of sea turtles are full of mysteries. Scientists, however, seem to have unscrambled one – the ability of turtles to find the sea moments after they hatch. Baby turtles are light-sensitive. In other words, they instinctively move toward a source of light. Some characteristic of the ocean – or of the sky over the ocean – guides young turtles to the sea. Under natural conditions, the seaward horizon is brighter than the landward horizon. That suggests that hatchling loggerheads find the ocean simply by rushing toward the brighter horizon. Artificial lights upset hatchling turtles' sense of direction and their means of finding the sea. By morning, turtles led astray by lights will be doomed by heat and a lack of moisture.

Even dark beaches are not without danger. Tiny loggerheads are bite-size snacks for raccoons and night herons, and they are no match for the claws of ghost crabs. Shells, streamers of seaweed, tidal wrack, and the ruts of vehicle tracks can be mountains and canyons for scrambling baby turtles.

Survivors of the hatch rush into the ocean. There they may be prey for such fish as mackerel, sharks, sea bass, and bluefish. The lucky ones presumably reach the great, floating mats of sargassum weed. There they can grow and hide until they become less attractive to ocean predators.

6 MYSTERIES OF THE LOGGERHEAD

Everyone loves a good mystery, and that may be one reason many scientists study sea turtles. Since nesting loggerheads are fairly common in the Southeast, researchers have measured and tagged thousands of them. Their nesting behavior is well known, but many mysteries swirl around the lives of loggerheads and other marine turtles at sea.

The primary reason for figuring out the mysteries associated with marine turtles is to assure the welfare of the turtles. Useful programs to protect turtles at sea cannot be planned until we know where they go, when they go there, and how long they stay. Are there places at sea where large numbers of loggerheads gather together? Where are their favorite feeding areas? At what age are they sexually mature? How are they affected by marine pollution?

Above:

Researchers flip a logger-head onto its back after nesting so that it can be easily measured and tagged.

From the moment that hatchling loggerheads enter the sea until the mature females swim ashore to nest some years later, the loggerheads' whereabouts are a puzzle. The best guess among scientists is that baby loggerheads hatched in the Southeast swim and drift as many as 100 miles into strong ocean currents such as the Gulf Stream. The little turtles become drifters in patches of sargassum weed. They live on tiny plants and animals.

Young loggerheads, roughly the size of plates, are found from time to time in lagoons, estuaries, creeks, and offshore waters. But where the turtles spend those first years reaching the size of dinner plates and how

37

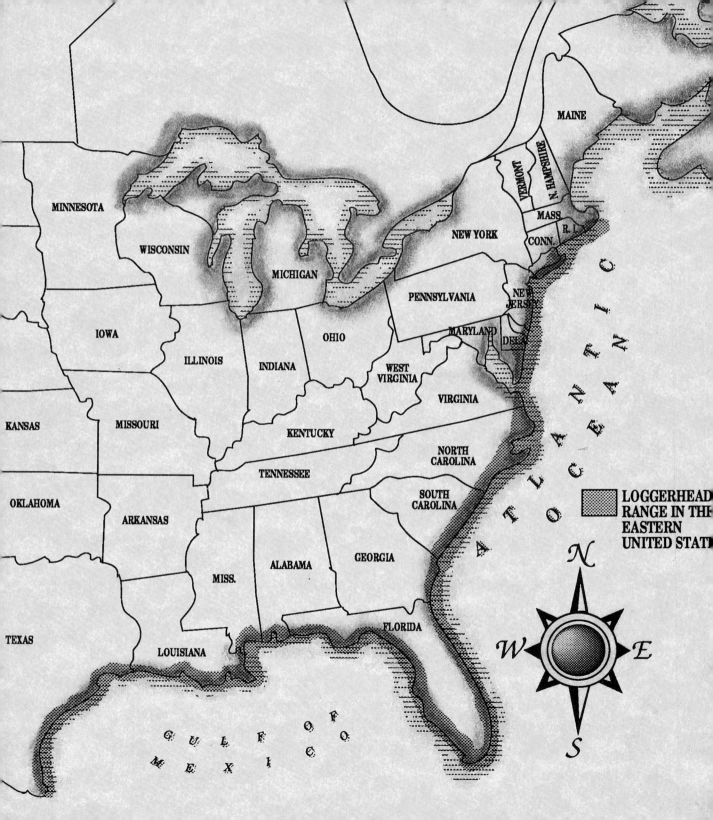

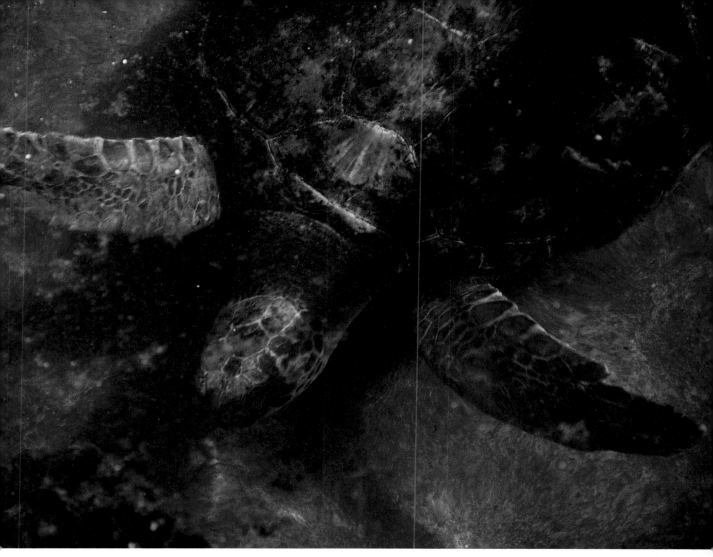

Above:
The mysteries of loggerheads and other marine turtles at sea are still waiting to be solved.

many years they spend in reaching that size remain in some doubt.

Turtles have a reputation for living to an old age, yet no one knows the average lifespan of a loggerhead. Dr. Richardson, who began studying loggerheads in Georgia in 1964, thinks "the typical loggerhead lives about 30 or 40 years – not hundreds as sometimes believed." Other scientists think that sea turtles grow so slowly that they aren't even capable of mating until they are 40 or 50 years old.

If the aging and travels of loggerheads are puzzling, they are no more puzzling than the loggerhead's ability to find its way back to a beach. Many scientists believe that adult female loggerheads usually return to the shore of their own birth to nest or to a nearby beach. Loggerheads are tagged so that scientists can learn about their travels when the tagged turtles are found later. Tag returns show that loggerheads often do return to the same beach where they nested before, but they have no way to prove those nesting turtles were born on the beaches where they nested.

How an adult loggerhead zeros in on the same nesting beach after hundreds of miles and several years of ocean travel is just another turtle mystery. An ability to "read" the stars in the night sky may play a part. Turtles, like salmon, may be somehow chemically imprinted to the smell of the home shore. Another possibility focuses on the special qualities of wave action of various shorelines.

A major problem in reading the travel log of a loggerhead exists. How can one safely tag or mark a hatchling in such a way that it will still carry the tag or mark in a recognizable way when it is a 225-pound adult?

7
FUTURE NIGHTS OF THE LOGGERHEAD

The important issue is whether loggerheads will be around to continue their summer journeys onto the night beaches. Perhaps as many as 20,000 loggerheads nested on Southeast beaches last summer, most of them on Florida's Atlantic coast. But in recent years this survivor from the Age of Dinosaurs has had to face more people, condominiums, and even vehicles on its nesting beaches. In oceans and bays it has had to deal with boats, nets and ocean **pollutants**.

Over the years, sea turtles have been hurt by the demands of fashion, greed, local tastes in food, and habitat destruction. All five groups of sea turtles are hunted in one place or another for their flesh and eggs. The green turtle has been a traditional favorite for its meat. The hawksbill has been hunted for meat and its strikingly beautiful shell. The most seriously endangered sea

turtle is the Atlantic ridley. In 1947, observers counted 40,000 nesting females at Rancho Nuevo, Mexico. Now there are 600, and the turtle's future is grim.

Loggerheads have not been hunted to the extent that some of their relatives have. They are not as tasty as green turtles, nor do they have the gorgeous shells of hawksbills. But in some parts of the world, such as the

Bahama Islands, loggerheads are taken for the table, and many coastal societies dig up loggerhead eggs. Like other sea turtles, loggerheads have also been hunted at one time or another for their oil and leather.

One of the loggerhead's greatest enemies in the Southeast has been the shrimp boat fleet. Active turtles need to surface for oxygen every few minutes. When sea turtles are swept into the nets dragged by shrimp boats, most of them are unable to swim to the surface for air. Before the nets are pulled aboard, the frantic turtles drown. Estimates of sea turtle deaths in shrimp nets in the Southeast ranged from 10,000 to 23,000 each year in the late 1980s. However, use of a turtle excluder device, known as a TED, on shrimp boat nets began in 1990. That may drastically reduce accidental drownings of sea turtles.

As recently as 1970, Florida docks handled nearly 500,000 pounds of sea turtles being processed for restaurants. But in the late 1970s, the United States became a leader in sea turtle conservation. All sea turtles in the United States are protected by provisions of the Endangered Species Act, and all are listed by the federal government as **endangered** or threatened. (The loggerhead is threatened, which means it could become endangered.) It is illegal to harm sea turtles on American beaches and in America's offshore waters. It is also illegal to import sea turtle products into the U.S.

The Endangered Species Act, passed by Congress, slammed shut the door on the rich American trade in turtle shells, leather, and meat. But in many countries the traffic in sea turtle products continues. A real challenge in sea turtle conservation is the need for international cooperation, the willingness of many countries to work together to protect the animals.

Left:

In the United States, where it has total protection, the loggerhead's future is fairly secure.

On a world-wide scale, the loggerhead's future is more promising than that of most of its relatives. Loggerheads are of little commercial value, and the species has the advantage of a broad range and widely scattered nest sites. Especially encouraging in the United States is the use of TEDs and the interest in sea turtle research. Several studies outside the U.S. are designed to find out if turtle farms and carefully managed harvests of turtles and eggs in developing countries will help save the animals in the long term. In addition, more and more countries seem willing to consider stronger positions on sea turtle conservation.

Meanwhile, the loggerhead has a stronghold – for the moment, at least – in the American Southeast while scientists probe its life history. They hope to find the lasting means to protect it in the United States and elsewhere.

GLOSSARY

adapted – having a characteristic of action, form, or behavior that improves a living thing's chances of survival in its habitat

barnacle – small, hard-shelled marine animals (crustaceans) that, as adults, are fixed to rocks, wood, shells, and other objects in the water

carapace – the upper shell of a turtle

carnivore – a meat eater

clutch – the eggs or babies in the nest of an egg-laying animal

endangered – in danger of becoming extinct

habitat – a plant or animal's immediate surroundings; its specific, preferred location

herbivorous – plant eating

herpetologist – a scientist whose specialty is the study of reptiles and amphibians

imprint – a process by which an animal develops an early recognition of something, such as a parent

marine – of or related to the ocean

odyssey – a long journey

omnivore – an animal that eats plant and animal material

ovipositor – a special exterior organ through which eggs pass from the body

parasite – an animal that lives on or in another animal and is harmful to the host animal

phosphorescence – a type of natural glow that can be seen at night

pollutant – poison or other harmful material that has been put into the environment

prey – an animal hunted for food by another animal

range – the entire area in which an animal might normally be found

reptiles – a group of cold-blooded animals with backbones, distinguished also by their covering of scales or hard, bony plates

wrack – the line of sea refuse that marks the highest reach of the tide

INDEX

Numbers in boldface type refer to photo and illustration pages.

Boaters sometimes see loggerhead turtles paddling in the open sea or in saltwater bays, usually along coastal Florida, Georgia, or South Carolina. Such sightings of loggerheads, however, are quite by chance. If you want to be certain to see a loggerhead, plan to visit a beach where loggerheads nest. Be sure your visit coincides with the summer nesting season.

Most of the loggerheads in the United States use beaches in the Southeast. On a summer night's walk along sandy beaches in South Carolina, Georgia, or Florida, you might find a nesting loggerhead. But the best way to see a loggerhead is to plan a visit to a Florida beach where groups are led on turtle walks for the purpose of observing turtles. Various organizations lead turtle walks, including the Nature Conservancy (Blowing Rocks Beach) and Florida Department of Parks and Recreation (Sebastian Inlet State Recreation Area). Always make a reservation in advance.

The likelihood of finding a nesting loggerhead in mid-summer is excellent on these turtle walks. The Atlantic beaches between Cape Canaveral and Jupiter Island are the best in the state for loggerhead observation.

Loggerhead Nesting Sites

Blowing Rocks Beach Preserve, Jupiter Island, FL
Manasota Key, Englewood, FL
Melbourne Beach, FL
Sanibel Island, FL
Sebastian Inlet State Recreation Area, FL

Ed. Note: Sites listed here do not represent *all* the places where nesting loggerheads may be observed. They do represent sites that are reliable and have relatively easy access.